Help Me, God, I'm a Working Mother!

Help Me, God, I'm a Working Mother!

Nancy B. Barcus

Judson Press ® Valley Forge

HELP ME, GOD, I'M A WORKING MOTHER!

Copyright © 1982
Judson Press, Valley Forge, PA 19481

All rights reserved. No part of this publication may be reproduced, stored in a retrieval system, or transmitted in any form or by any means, electronic, mechanical, photocopying, recording, or otherwise, without the prior permission of the copyright owner, except for brief quotations included in a review of the book.

Unless otherwise indicated, the Scripture quotations in this publication are from the Revised Standard Version of the Bible copyrighted 1946, 1952 © 1971, 1973 by the Division of Christian Education of the National Council of Churches of Christ in the U.S.A., and used by permission.

Other quotations of the Bible are from:
  HOLY BIBLE New International Version, copyright © 1978, New York International Bible Society. Used by permission.

Library of Congress Cataloging in Publication Data
Barcus, Nancy B.
  Help me, God, I'm a working mother!

  1. Mothers—Prayer-books and devotions—English.
2. Mothers—Employment. I. Title.
BV4529.B36   242'.6431   82-98
ISBN 0-8170-0954-X   AACR2

The name JUDSON PRESS is registered as a trademark in the U.S. Patent Office. Printed in the U.S.A.

To Heidi, Jeff, and Hans
who make me a working mother.
Thank you.

"But I don't want to work."
"Sure you do. You'll love it."

So often we have to be convinced to work the first time around. The thought of being a working woman, let alone a working mother, severely upsets our once carefully cultivated image of the future. So we may be surprised when we end up behind a desk somewhere. And we may be even more surprised when we like it.

I found myself at work at nine in the morning two weeks after my first protest. Doubtful of the wisdom of my being there, I sat behind a gray metal desk with matching file cabinet in an office of thirty-five experienced women.

"Just file these for a while and ask questions when you get stuck."

"These" were orders for cardboard boxes—hundreds of them, in all sizes—destined for the best stores on every Fifth Avenue in the country. My job: to pull out the RUSH orders from the rest and hurry them downstairs to the plant manager.

Soon I was the fastest box-orderer on the floor and, more important than that, I found I was enjoying the work. As a bonus I had dozens of stories to take home at night—the elderly red-wigged woman who clicked her teeth, the bearded machine operator in the lunchroom who read Greek mythology with his peanut butter sandwich, the unending number of secretaries planning their weddings in loud voices which he never seemed to hear as he turned the pages.

That was the beginning. Now it is hard to imagine not working.

Being a mother complicates my life—it means I lead two lives like every working mother in the country. Once the children "arrive," the job of mothering is irrevocable. The job behind the desk may be irrevocable, too. If there is no choice but to lead two lives or if our choice is to lead two lives, we learn to adjust our lives in accordance with this double employment.

This book is about those adjustments. It searches out the angles of surprise—and moments of praise to God—that come to working mothers who see beyond those adjustments to the grace of Christ: "My grace is sufficient for thee . . ." (2 Corinthians 12:9).

Sometimes I wonder, "Shall I keep going with this life?" The three busy children in our household cheer me on. I am a working mother for numbers of reasons, and I don't mind saying that I like it better every year. In fact, my son must like it too. "Next time we move," he says, "I hope you won't stay home and be one of those ordinary mothers."

My Latchkey Kid

My ten-year-old son can't be persuaded to take off his key even when I'm home. A child wearing a latchkey is supposed to be the sign of a bad mother; so I wish he wouldn't wear it all around the neighborhood even on weekends.

He is proud of it. It makes him a man, his eyes say, when I ask him to take it off. His words are, "Aw, Mom, it's cool."

So I tuck it down inside his shirt where it won't show and say, "Okay."

Then when I look at him racing sideways past me through the family room to where his bicycle leans against the porch, I see the bright three-inch key dangling outside his shirt again. It swings from the sturdy chain I bought him after the first two broke. It is made of strong little beads and looks like a bathtub chain or an army dog-tag chain.

"All right. Wear it," I sigh to myself so that he can't hear. "Let the whole neighborhood see it."

Looking out the kitchen window, I see him kick up his bicycle stand with all the earnestness of my husband at the lawn mower. He is thinking what a man he is. "Like my dad. With my own key."

On his bright green shirt the brass key stands out like an ornament. It partially covers up the face of the Incredible Hulk stamped on the shirtfront so that you can't see the face clearly. The key is more important.

I watch him zooming down the street, the proudly worn chain flapping and the wind blowing his yellow hair.

Funny thing about that key. Since he's been wearing it, he makes his bed in the morning and even brushes his teeth. He shuts the dog in the kitchen before he gets on the bus in the morning, and he lets the dog out again at three-thirty in the afternoon when he gets home. He even remembers to hang the key on its hook at night so that it will be there in the morning. (Well, most of the time.)

The main thing about the key, though, is that he knows I will not take it back. The key is evidence that I trust him. In that trust is the key's main importance. There is a further message in the key, too, which one day he will understand. The key, given in trust, is a working mother's benediction:

Thou, therefore, my son, be strong in the grace that is in Christ Jesus (2 Timothy 2:1).

That Baby-Sitter Reads Better Than You, Mom

"She read three whole chapters an' she never stopped." Blue-eyed Heidi greeted me at the door with this news, barring my steps.

My feet tired from the long walk up the hill, I sagged against the door and smiled at the twenty-year-old college girl who spent her afternoons in my kitchen. She didn't even look tired after reading three chapters of Raggedy Ann. One chapter was my top limit.

"She taught me a song, too." Heidi turned a somersault on the rug as I sat down inside the door and took off my shoes.

"There was a crooked man an' he went a crooked mile,
He found a crooked sixpence upon a crooked . . ."

"Yes, yes," I said to cut her off, then stopped. I could at least let her finish.

When Heidi's voice finally sounded the last note, I stood up, shoes in hand.

"See you tomorrow, Heidi," Valerie said and bounded out the door, too energetic for five o'clock.

Looking through the archway to where I would set the table, I could see on the dining room table five paintings lined up to dry. Five pairs of wide, black shoe-button eyes stared out from five red and blue Raggedy Anns.

"Like those, Mom? I did this one an' this one."

I could tell which ones but I didn't say so.

"Valerie's fun."

I could see that.

"She reads better'n you. You know that, Mom?"

Heidi hauled herself up to the kitchen counter as I headed back toward the pantry and took out a package of spaghetti. She eyed me until I answered. Even when I'd stayed at home all day, I hadn't done all that they had done in one afternoon. "Yes," I said, too reluctantly.

"But I'm hungry now. You make good spaghetti."

Subject closed.

I opened the cupboard.

"Glad you're home," she said.

That's all the praise I needed for one day.

For I say, through the grace given unto me, to every man that is among you, not to think of himself more highly than he ought to think; but to think soberly, according as God hath dealt to every man the measure of faith. Having then gifts differing according to the grace that is given to us . . . (Romans 12:3, 6a).

Please Don't Be Sick Today

On a day with five things more than usual to do at work, someone in a family of three children may decide to be sick. "It's my stomach," or "Oh, my head!" are the usual complaints.

If the temperature is over 101° and your child is under ten, it's a day at home for both of you. If the child is older, steady telephone calls all day long—coaching-by-wire—work just as well. But a younger child, just mildly sick, may get to go to work with you or with Father. Usually with you.

"Hi. I'm sick today," he smiles to the receptionist as he first steps off the elevator to your office.

"That's too bad. How are you feeling?"

"Pretty awful. Got any pretzels?"

"No. Sorry." She smiles at him as I turn away.

"Well, the pop machine, then. Just give me some change, Mom, and I'll be okay."

"He's cute," the receptionist says.

I hand him the change and unlock my office door, shrugging for a reply. Cute, maybe, but not what I needed today.

I'm scheduled for three conference meetings in the next two hours, and one of them has kept me awake all night planning what to say. How do you tell the boss not to mind if you're not as organized as usual today?

I tell my son, who returns with a can of cherry pop, to sit at my desk and draw while I go to the first meeting. He can lie on the sofa across the hall if he feels worse, I tell him.

"Sure." He's already drawing dive bombers on my memo pad and has three finished by the time I'm back for something I forgot.

"I'm bored."

"Lunch in two hours. Lie down."

"Wish I'd stayed home."

I wish he had, too. I don't say it.

He knocks on the conference room door during my second meeting. "Almost done?"

"No."

I'm in the middle of giving a report. I smile as the door closes, clear my throat, and go on. My colleagues smile, too. They don't mind, they say. He's a nice boy, they say.

At lunchtime I go back to get him. He is at the reception desk learning to operate the switchboard and finishing a pack of peanuts.

I go to my office and open the file cabinet to put away my papers. A sign taped to the top drawer says, "Danger. Killer Mouse Inside."

In the hallway my boss passes and smiles.

My son bounds toward me and slips his hand into mine. "I'd like a cheeseburger and fries, and I'm so glad I came."

Out on the street I'm going over the meeting in my head and missing a story about Spiderman. I wasn't at my best today but it was nice of Mr. Flanagan to act like it was all right anyhow.

"When I grow up, if I can't be an astronaut, maybe I'll be like Mr. Flanagan. I bet he could fly if he took off his glasses. . . ."

I feel the tight grip on my hand. It's days like this, not the ordinary days, that I'll remember later on.

. . . in every thing by prayer and supplication with thanksgiving let your requests be made known unto God. And the peace of God, which passeth all understanding, shall keep your hearts and minds through Christ Jesus (Philippians: 4:6-7).

Never Mind, I'll Do It Myself

In the hallway stood my daughter, holding out her favorite blouse to me. "It's been three days," she said. "I asked you to fix it Monday."

"I'll do it Friday," I said. Behind me the clock struck six-thirty in the morning. At seven-thirty my bus would be at the corner.

For an answer she dropped the blouse on the floor and gave it a little kick. Its navy blue sleeves picked up lint and dust where I hadn't run the mop yet.

"Pick it up, please," I said.

"It's dirty now." She lifted it up. "I'll just toss it in there." With a swift pitch she aimed it straight into the wicker laundry hamper.

In the bedroom my husband was quietly folding his socks into flat neat piles. He appeared in the hallway where we stood.

"You shouldn't have done that," he said to her. "Come here."

She followed him to our bedroom. He opened a bureau drawer and took out a large needle.

"You got your sewing badge in Girl Scouts," he said. "Let's

see what the badge is worth."

I left them alone together before she got the thread through the needle's eye. Getting pancakes ready downstairs would be more restful than watching this procedure.

I listened for the sounds of shouting and whining from upstairs, but none came. I made the pancakes a little more slowly than usual, then took the meat out of the freezer to thaw for supper. Still no sound.

"Pancakes," I called up to them and listened for their feet coming down, wondering if I'd called in time to prevent disaster.

"Look what I did." I heard her voice before I saw them.

As they rounded the corner, I could see that my daughter had her favorite blouse on and was twisting the button between her fingers in case I could not tell which one she had fixed. If she twisted it any more, it would come off.

"Good," I nodded. I wondered if she knew how good.

"He never even yelled at me."

"Good again," I said, looking at his calm face. How had he done it?

"Know what?"

I wasn't sure I could stand any more surprises so early in the morning, but I answered her, "No. Tell me."

She fastened her eyes on me and said the words slowly, glancing back at her father just once.

"Next time I think I'll just do it myself."

I wondered if she understood what a good thing she had said. All this time I'd thought folding socks and sewing on buttons were my job. I would need some help learning to accept my family's self-sufficiency.

As we stood together, I thought of the verse they had demonstrated:

Bear ye one another's burdens, and so fulfil the law of Christ (Galatians 6:2).

It's Okay to Be a Grown-up, Mom

"Andrea's mom talks on the phone all day." My daughter's voice is full of amazement. "She had on this white tennis dress, and she was lying on the floor with her feet up on a chair, laughing like one of my high school friends. She was on the phone an hour."

"Really?"

"Yes. And do you know what she said when she hung up?"

I wait, raising my eyebrows.

"She said, 'I just have to get a maid. I can't keep up with all this housework.'"

"Sounds like a good life," I say, laughing.

"Oh, no," she replies. "It would be boring, don't you think?"

Of course I think so.

I remember the restless days before I worked, my mind casting about for direction and worrying about the perpetual household duties.

Now that I work, I notice that my household is neither cleaner nor dirtier than it was when I had all that time to fret about it. Being on a schedule has made me more efficient and organized than I ever pictured—I know what has to be done and when, and my mind runs on several tracks at once. It's almost uncanny what I catch my mind doing to keep up with things. I wouldn't trade all this energy and bustle today for one slow afternoon of wishing for something interesting to do.

The children—three of them—have their regular jobs now around the house: vacuuming, dusting, folding the laundry, and other useful recreation is divided among them. I'm not fretting out loud anymore about the perpetual chores of running a household. Most days, with some slip-ups, we run it together.

When we're on top of things, which is more days than not, we all make our own beds, clear off our own plates, keep crumbs away from the television, put our own clothes in the laundry hamper. Things work about as well as when I did them all myself all day long, my mind restless and searching.

"Andrea's mother is like a little girl."

My daughter breaks in on my thoughts. Her voice is filled with urgency. "I'm glad you're a grown-up."

For God hath not given us the spirit of fear; but of power, and of love, and of a sound mind (2 Timothy 1:7).

Late for Dinner

"I fixed dinner tonight!"

I'm an hour late. I called ahead to warn everybody, but being late throws everything off, me included.

Hans has the table set, though—the forks and knives reversed—and has a boldly lettered menu laid out in the middle of the table. It's written with a black Magic Marker on the back of a math paper:

    HOT DOGS
    LETUCE (with one T)
    WATER OR MILK

Nobody likes hot dogs much. They're emergency fare or lunchtime specialties, but it's his first time as chef, and Hans has decided to do it all on his own.

At ten years of age, he can reach the stove without pulling anything over on himself, remember to turn off the flame, and even wipe up the counters if he's reminded. I hope he remembers. This is his night to be boss, and it wouldn't do for me to nag about the mess.

The catsup bottle sits in the middle of the table, and he's

poured five glasses of milk which are getting warm. Two of us don't drink milk, but we will tonight.

"Reach me those plates up there," he says. "They're too high."

I'll have to move them lower if he decides he likes this venture well enough to try again.

"Now sit down. I'll serve."

We take our places around the table. Hans needs a little help getting plates from the stove to the table; so he asks his dad. Then he sits down, beaming at his plate, and pours on the extra catsup before we pray. We give thanks. Then he wipes his fingers across his lap and licks them.

We eat our hot dogs and our salad as if they're the best we've ever had.

"You did great," I tell him.

He smiles and says, "I know it."

After supper I let him run off, a child again. He's all worn out.

I clean up after him. The stove is spattered, and the counters have thin wedges of butter smudged across them from buttering the rolls.

I wipe off what I can, and I notice cooky dough on some of the drawer handles and down the cupboards from the last time Heidi baked cookies. Some of it is dried on and needs the SOS treatment.

The price of letting them learn for themselves, I remind myself, is to be tolerant of the extra stickiness in my work space. They'll get older and wipe up better. I'm working hard at learning not to mention these things at the wrong time if I can help myself, though the stickiness bothers me.

However, today is a first. It's more important that Hans did something for all of us and for his mother, who was late.

Above all these things put on charity, which is the bond of perfectness (Colossians 3:14).

Celebration for a Clean Face

I could never get my son out of the house in the morning *clean* until I started working. Before that, each morning he would look as though he'd forgotten that he had any hair to comb or a face to be swept clean of the half-moon of dried milk still on it from bedtime. Ten minutes before the bus came, he would be sitting in his room dreaming or sneaking a look at a TV cartoon with the volume turned very low or handling his spaceship just one more time.

The bus would be half a minute from the corner, and I'd catch sight of him pulling his shirt over his touseled head and grabbing his shoes in his hand—"to put them on when I get my seat on the bus."

I've found only two remedies. *One* is to let him miss the bus and be very late for school, an embarrassment in which his teachers fully cooperate. *Two,* and far preferable, is to tell him—as I have had to do—that he is now his own manager. He must get himself ready and out of the house on his own because my bus leaves ten minutes before his bus arrives.

I watched his expression when I first told him. It said: No mother hovering in the background and looking at her watch to keep me moving? That thought has spurred him to get himself up, dressed, and down for breakfast minutes before he'd even stirred his sleepy head before. He smiles that even, white alertness of a smile and wears his favorite shirt as often as I can keep it washed. After breakfast he brushes his teeth without my mentioning it and slicks his hair down a bit too much with a wet brush. He leaves a wet washrag on the sink to prove his face-washing diligence.

"Don't worry. I've got my key," he calls out as he packs his red nylon backpack with his homework papers and the bag lunch I've made. He looks pleased with himself as I say good-bye.

I wonder as I leave if he minds my leaving the house a few minutes before him. He was only nine years old when I first left him, and he is still the last one out; the other two children are already on an early bus. But he ignores my leaving as if it is of small consequence compared to all he has done so far this morning and compared to the busy day he's anticipating. Never once do I think he might throw his arms around me at the door and say, "Don't leave."

In retrospect, sitting on the bus at seven-thirty-five, I recall the frantic details of his old habits: his racing out the door, shoes in hand, sometimes forgetting his lunch. What a distressing start for a day that must have been, I think.

Now he is calm and organized and cheerful, watching the clock so that he can pull the door shut behind him and be at the bus stop five minutes early.

It's a better start of the day for both of us. Neither of us is frantic and frustrated, needing a whole hour to calm down from the stress of two intelligent people, mother and son, trying to maneuver him, like a stalled tank, out the door.

The bus hums beneath me and I shut my eyes and smile. I see the clean boy riding bus #45 just a few miles behind me. I suspect his socks may not match way up under his Wrangler jeans but he'll get good at that another year. Meanwhile, we're on our way.

My son, if your heart is wise, then my heart will be glad . . . (Proverbs 23:15, NIV).

Did You Say "Organized"?

"But how can you keep your house *organized* when you're gone all day?"

That's a hard one. Yet some of my friends who are home all day aren't organized either.

Organized means dishes done and beds made by nine o'clock.

Organized means the house looking fit for a surprise visitor at any moment of the day.

Organized means knowing what you'll have for supper more than an hour before it's time to eat.

Actually, being home all day tempts me to let those things—dishes, beds, meal plans—wait until later. Being out of the house by seven-thirty means I've got no choice. Funny how it's easier to make the bed when you first get up, easier to rinse and stack the dishes before the egg dries hard on them, easier to take the meat for supper out of the freezer in the morning or even place it in the oven and have someone turn on the oven after school.

As for having the house ready for visitors—it's not until we come home at night that the blitz begins. Then visitors must take their chances. It begins with shoes at the back door and coats dropped quickly in transit to the telephone which is ringing frantically.

The real undoing of a neat house, whether I've been at home or away, is when the mail gets opened and the homework begins. Heidi studies best when her papers are spread across the floor in front of the fireplace, she says. We can expect an apple core somewhere and maybe a gum wrapper—to be picked up later, she promises. She'll leave a letter downstairs, too, if the mail has been good to her. When three children are doing homework or answering the phone according to their own quirks, it's best for a visitor to be brave. By bedtime or the following morning very early when I'm alert, we can have it all put back again—the house ready and quiet all day long—until we come home once more.

I call that *organized* because it works for us. We know when to be particular and when to close our eyes. At least I'm trying to remember that lesson. It makes living together, whether I'm at home or away, a far more peaceful venture.

Now the Lord of peace himself give you peace always by all means (2 Thessalonians 3:16).

A Plea for Safety

It's four o'clock. One hour to go. My phone is ringing.
"Hi, Ma. I'm home. Can I ride my bike?"
"*May,* not *can,*" I say. "May."
"Sure. Okay. Thanks. See ya."
"Wait," I say.
"Yeah?"
"Be careful."
"Oh, Mom!"

I hang up. Across town my ten-year-old is wheeling his new BM-X bike with the bright red metal spokes and handlebar brakes out of the garage. In a minute he will be lined up at the end of the street—not a busy street—for a race. Will he slip on a piece of gravel, "pop a wheelie" at the wrong moment, maybe draw blood on his elbow or his chin while I'm not there to know it?

I think of the wind slapping into his face on this warm spring afternoon, the grass a light green and just coming up, the yellow forsythia along the fences. In the sunshine as his spirits soar, he has discarded his jacket. I know it though I'm not there to see it. I wonder if he is winning the race and if his face is red with eagerness as his hair stands straight in the gusty air. Ask him today if life is fine and good.

Of course he does not fall. Why am I so certain that he will? I close my eyes by my office telephone and pray for him for the hundredth time this month.

He is already a patchwork of stitches: eight above his eyebrow, three on his lip, two below his nose, four on his chin. I was at home with him for every fall that required those stitches. I was standing right next to him when he fell off the chair and put his teeth through his tongue. He'll fall, I remind myself, when he's ready to—whether I'm there or not.

That's comfort. But he's not replaceable; so I pray again. I know, trusting him to be sensible today, the real value of a human life. The price of trust. And I'm reminding myself now that God knows the value of him even more than I.

For he shall give his angels charge over thee, to . . . bear thee up . . . lest thou dash thy foot against a stone (Psalm 91:11-12).

Suppertime Panic

What'll I fix for supper? It's five-thirty and I'm all out of flour.

Heidi's been cooking again. I can tell because the oil is gone, too, and there's only a half cup of sugar left. I especially need the flour for biscuits. There's nothing to do but borrow from a neighbor—bless God for them—and remind Heidi to keep a list.

I look first, out of curiosity, into the pan sitting on the stove. I lift the lid. It's a good thing I did. She's made macaroni.

I cancel the biscuit idea and the trip to the neighbor. I heat up the fry pan for minute steaks and start a salad. In spite of using up my supplies, Heidi has solved my problem.

Through the opened cupboard door, I see a plate of oatmeal cookies. The flour culprits. The oatmeal is probably gone, too. But I remind myself that she fixed the macaroni without asking anyone for help. That's a lot more than I could do at twelve.

I look at my kitchen counter, smudged with shortening. I see cookie dough along the seams in the drawers. I try not to look at the bowls and beaters in the sink. I'd left the kitchen absolutely clear this morning. I'll have to show her how to clean up.

I really hate the mess. It hurts me down inside. She doesn't even see it, I can tell. I call her.

"Heidi," I say nicely (I hope). "Can you wipe that up, please?" I point to the smudges on the drawers.

"Where?"

I point again.

"Oh, that."

She grabs a clean dish towel from the drawer and swabs the counters and the drawers, then wipes out the crusty mixing bowl with it.

"A clean towel," I moan. "Please don't take a new one next time."

"Oh. Sorry. It'll wash." She tosses it into the laundry room. A clean towel, dirty in two minutes.

Her macaroni is heating up too much. I grab it quickly to preserve it from burning.

"Thanks for the macaroni," I say and try to forget about the towel.

"Sure," she says. "Next time I think I'll make spaghetti."

Spaghetti. That will mean tomato sauce dried all over the stove. All her cooking means extra work for me, but one day it will be helpful to have this daughter in the kitchen taking care of things. I vow not to mind the smudges and spilled sugar; I have to vow it several times a week and even bite my tongue.

Next week she'll make the spaghetti if I don't discourage her. And after that, who knows? I do want her to be independent. So I say out loud to her, still standing there and waiting for me to finish my daydreaming, "Yes, make the spaghetti. That will be great. I'll love it."

I turn back to the stove and rescue the minute steaks just in time. I hope, as I turn them over, that she will be a better cook than I am.

. . . do not embitter your children, or they will become discouraged (Colossians 3:21).
Bear with each other and forgive whatever grievances you may have against one another . . .
And over all these virtues put on love, which binds them all together in perfect unity (Colossians 3:13-14).

God Bless the Neighbors

"I missed the bus this morning, Mom."

"Uh-huh," I say absently and then start to listen. By the time Hans missed the bus, I was well on my way to work. There was nothing I could have done to help.

"What did you do?" I ask, listening hard now.

His mouth is full; so I have to wait until he swallows his milk. He's in no hurry to tell me; so I relax. He doesn't seem upset. He sets his glass down.

"Mrs. Henderson took me. I knocked on her door and told her, and she took me with her coat over her pajamas and her curlers still on."

Mrs. Henderson. We borrow eggs from her, potatoes, yeast, and even a utensil to unstop the disposal when bones catch in it. She smiles and laughs, and likes to talk when we go over as if she had plenty of time to be nice. She's the best neighbor on the block.

I wonder how she always has whatever we've run out of while the kids are baking cookies. I wonder how she's always so cheerful and willing to be interrupted. She's always the same, however she manages it, as if being a good neighbor is the thing she enjoys best. We even leave an extra house key in her kitchen in case someone forgets a key in the morning and can't get in after school.

"I hope you said thank you," I finally say to Hans as he resumes his supper.

He nods. "Sure," he says. "But she always says 'That's all right,' and smiles before I even finish saying it."

"Great," I say. "Keep saying thank you. We couldn't function without a neighbor like her, could we?"

"No," he says. "She even put the dog in last week when he ran away from me before school. She saw him in the snow and she called him. She used our key to put him in the house."

I hadn't heard that before. After supper I call her to thank her for both favors.

"Hi, Helen. I hear you've been a good neighbor again."

"Oh, yes," she says. "Did Hans tell you how funny I looked? Tell him I'll try to look better next time."

"Next time? Oh, Helen. I hope there won't be a next time." I add, "You were super to take him."

"That's okay," she says. "You just call me. I don't mind. Anytime."

"You're terrific," I say. "How could we function without a good neighbor like you?"

"You would," she says. "It wasn't much."

"It was, too," I insist. "Every working mother needs a neighbor like you."

Helen just laughs. I hang up, thoughtful. Without the support of people like Helen, how would we do it? "Thanks, Lord," I whisper. "Don't let her move away." I remember how many times her husband has been transferred and know that could happen again any time.

And this commandment have we from him, That he who loveth God love his brother also (1 John 4:21).

Helping Hands

A maid. The thought rolls around in my mind like a piece of fresh apple pie.

It's Saturday, and abandoned socks lie in two or three corners from a late and hasty Friday bedtime. A long web of filmy dust hangs from the brass chandelier in the dining room. The sliding glass doors to the backyard glint in the morning sun with fresh handprints, too many to count. I take another sip of coffee and dream of it again. A maid.

But that's a luxury I can't manage. Things are already too expensive—three growing children; three sets of music lessons; all the expenses of school, dentists, sports equipment, football games. Well, it won't do, not for me. Besides, I'm too independent to accept someone else's work—but that's another problem. A maid is out of the question.

I sip more coffee. The idea comes to me in the morning quiet all of a sudden. I have three maids, living right in my house, ages ten, twelve, and fourteen on their last birthdays. They're fairly smart, their report cards say. They can do something to help, I'm sure of it.

I decide to announce the idea next Friday, and I make a

list—nine jobs to divide among them: vacuum upstairs, vacuum down, dust, clean the stairs, empty wastebaskets, fold laundry, pick the bathtub, toilet, or sink to scrub. I wonder what they'll choose.

Ten-year-old Hans proves good at the stairs and the vacuuming and elects scrubbing the toilet for some reason. I remember a married couple who wrote a book about sharing the grubby jobs equally, and I think Hans may be on his way to a good marriage. Twelve-year-old Jeff scrubs the sink, empties the wastebaskets, and also vacuums. Heidi dusts the bric-a-brac with deftness, folds the laundry but despises scrubbing the tub, threatening to trade it to Hans.

After a month's trial, the proposition seems to be working. I can't believe it but why shouldn't I?

I've got time for the fingerprints on the windows, scrubbing the kitchen floor, and dusting all the little corners I've been noticing with despair. If company should drop in on a Saturday afternoon, we'd look fine. By Sunday night, though, I wish that the children hadn't left schoolbooks in front of the TV, towels dragging on the floor, and more socks in the corner. Still, we've made a start. By the time we all leave the house on Monday, if we set the alarm, we can pick up in the early morning and get the beds made. The house will make it through another week, without a maid. Or, better yet, with three of them.

. . . *thy children [shall be] like olive plants round about thy table (Psalm 128:3b).*

Long-Distance Doctoring

"I've got a fever."

I feel Jeff's head. He does. One hundred and one degrees, I'll bet. I can tell because he's still in bed. Jeff is always up before I am. He's the one who's ready to leave while the rest of us are still combing our hair once again. He hates to be late, he says. Today he's not going anywhere.

"I'll just stay here," he whispers. "I'm not hungry either."

"What do you want to do?" I say.

It's the first time he has been sick since I started the new job and the first time since he has turned twelve.

"I'll be okay," he says. "Just let me stay here."

"Do you want me to stay, too?" I feel his forehead again.

"Naw."

I take his temperature. "Just what I thought. One hundred and one."

"It's a bug," he says. "Rusty had it yesterday. The whole school's got it."

"Tell you what," I say. "Why don't you come downstairs and sleep on the sofa. You can watch TV if you feel better and you'll be near the phone for me to call."

TV all day long. Hans would have loved the chance. Jeff isn't so excited by cartoons and quiz shows anymore. He just nods and limps down to the sofa, carrying his pillow. I turn on the TV and he shuts his eyes.

It's late; so I dress quickly and give the other two children cereal for breakfast instead of the ritual pancakes.

"'Bye, Jeff," I say at the door. He opens his eyes, then shuts them again.

At ten o'clock I call him. The phone rings eleven times before he finally answers. His voice is slow. "H'lo?"

"How're you doing?"

"Fine." He whispers it. Not fine.

"Drink any orange juice?"

"No. Not hungry."

"Well, did you take the aspirin I left?"

"Yeah."

"Okay. Then go on back to sleep. I'll call back at noon."

At noon his voice is more alert. "Do you have any Coke around?" he asks. The aspirin is working, I decide.

"Ginger ale. In the refrigerator. Hidden in the back."

"Gone," he says.

"Gone? All thirty-two ounces?" I'm curious. "It was there this morning."

"Gone," he says again.

"You're better," I say. "Try the orange juice now."

I hear him sigh as I put the phone down. I write "ginger ale" on my memo pad. Jeff is taking good care of himself. I relax and remember that he's just a phone call away. I pray for him.

Do not be anxious about anything, but in everything, by prayer and petition, with thanksgiving, present your requests to God (Philippians 4:6, NIV).

Trust or Nothing

"Can I go to Rusty's after school?" It's Jeff on the phone.
"If his mother is home. Sure."
"His mother works."
"Oh-oh. Guess you can't, Jeff."
"Guess he can't come over to our house, either?"
"No. Sorry."

I hear him hang up the phone reluctantly, and I imagine the sad look on his face. Jeff is the one with the sad eyes, telling all without a word. It isn't fun to tell the neighborhood children they can't come in because your parents aren't home.

My phone rings again. "Hi. It's me. Long time, huh?"
"Hi." I listen. He doesn't sound too unhappy.
"We're going to the pool."
"Great." I bought summer memberships at the pool, three of them, and the kids have hardly used them. I'd hoped they would swim away the warm weather. Why don't they ever do the expected?
"Call me when you get home," I add.

He's gone before I finish my sentence. I worry about him. Will he really go to the pool? Will he meet the right kids there?

Is he telling me what he's really doing? I wonder if every working mother today worries, too.

Jeff calls me finally.

"How was the pool?" I ask.

"Boring."

I'm quiet. What can I say?

"But we stayed there anyway. Honest, we did. And we bought a soda on the way home at the store. Rusty's gone to do his paper route. Guess I'll try a few shots with the basketball."

"See you soon," I say. "Tell Sis to boil some potatoes."

"Okay."

"And, Jeff, thanks for checking it all out with me. You could have done anything. How would I know? I can only keep this up—this working—because I believe you."

"Aw, sure," he said. "I wouldn't dare cheat on you. If you had to quit work, how would I get my allowance!"

"You're talking now," I say, chuckling. I'd tap him lightly on the shoulder if I were there, admiring the sparks of mirth in his eyes.

"See ya," he says.

"Be good," I say, then bite my tongue. I've said enough. Now I pray for him.

My son, if sinners entice thee, consent thou not. Whoso hearkeneth unto me shall dwell safely, and shall be quiet from fear of evil (Proverbs 1:10, 33).

 Emergency

"I did something terrible today, Mother."

I look at his face and my heart plummets. Hans's eyes are round and ready to cry if I decide to be angry. What could a ten-year-old do that would be so alarming?

"I ate the inside of a tennis ball."

His eyes are still solemn.

I want to say, "Is that all?" and I want to laugh, but I do neither.

"Do you think it was poison?" he asks me. "Billy said it was made of poison."

"It's just rubber," I say. "Go get the ball and let me see it. Why would you do that anyway?"

He hands me the peeled-back ball, and I see that he's hardly chewed anything off the center. Probably did it for a dare.

"Will I die?" he asks. "Will I?"

"Not this time," I say. "But I'm not happy about it. Why did you do it?"

"Billy told me to. He said I was a sissy unless I did it."

Billy. Fifteen pounds lighter than Hans. Can't kick a football halfway across the yard. I look at Hans's strong arms and shoulders and sturdy knees and wonder why a little boy that he could push down in a minute could exert such power of suggestion over him.

"You're no sissy," I say. (I don't add the part about pushing the other boy down if he wants to.)

"I know I'm not," he says.

"Then why?"

"So the kids wouldn't laugh at me."

"Oh? Do they laugh at you?"

"No. But they might."

"Hans," I plead. "You're not making sense. Why would you do something that could make you die—for no reason—even if you *were* wrong about it's being dangerous."

"I was dumb," he says. "Just dumb. I'm sorry."

"Great," I say. "That's true that you were dumb. But the trouble is, how do I know you won't do something else stupid? Do I have to follow you around like a private eye?"

"Aw, Mom," he says. "Don't worry. I'm only dumb once in a while. You know me better than that."

"I thought I did."

"You still do. I just slipped, that's all."

"No more?"

"I told you, didn't I?"

Yes. He told me. It's his honesty that will save us all. I close my eyes right in front of him and thank God for him.

Then I say, "Be careful, won't you? God broke the pattern after he made you. You're the only one he's got."

He gives the bright, even grin and heads for his bike.

Hold thou me up, and I shall be safe: and I will have respect unto thy statutes continually (Psalm 119:117).
Teach me knowledge and good judgment, for I believe in your commands. Before I was afflicted I went astray, but now I obey your word (Psalm 119:66-67, NIV).

Locked Out

"I lost my key."

The news brings the family operation to a halt. Without keys we're out of business.

"Lost it? Where?" It's the first question to ask.

"Don't know. Or how would it be lost?"

"Think, then. Where did you last have it?" I look up at the nail beside the kitchen door where the key is supposed to be hanging. Empty. Hans shakes his head.

"Use Jeff's then."

We look at Jeff. His face is blank. He shakes his head, too. "He's been letting me in with *his*." He nods at Hans.

"Where's yours?"

Jeff makes a gesture with his hands to say he doesn't know. "Haven't seen it for a long time."

I don't know whether to let the revelation speak for itself or to offer a lecture. I choose silence. My lecture would not sound rational or well planned.

"Heidi's, then. You'll have to use hers. You're home first. Take her key, then give it back to her when she gets home."

I think I've solved the problem for now. Heidi thinks not.

"Not my key. Nobody borrows my key. He'll lose it." She nods at him and Hans flinches at the truth. "I'm not letting him take *my* key and lose it." Her voice is definite.

Under the table he kicks her. She's a big girl but she yells anyway. Still she has her point. The one who loses the key is the one who sits outside. That's what we said when we first gave out the keys. Hans will have a forty-five-minute wait until Heidi's bus comes. I explain that calmly, not mentioning the kick under the table.

"I'm staying after school today," Heidi says. "I won't be home until five. Hans will be sitting outside a long time."

Jeff says, "I have football. I won't need a key. It's okay if mine is lost. I mean . . . well, no, it's not okay. Sorry."

Hans's face is white. Sitting outside on the porch from three-thirty until five o'clock, especially while his bike is locked in the garage, seems a perilous retribution.

If Heidi were coming home at four, I'd let him wait it out. Half an hour, even forty-five minutes, is exactly the right amount of time to jog him into remembering his key next time. That is, when we find it. But an hour and a half? No way!

"Tell you what," I say. "Give me your key, Heidi. Hans won't lose it this way. We'll leave it over at the Hendersons'. After school he can unlock the door and leave the key on the counter. You can pick it up as soon as you come in the door."

Heidi hands her key over as if she'll never see it again. "It better be on the counter," she says.

"It will," I promise, staring significantly at Hans. He nods. "Now run it over to Mrs. Henderson before I have to leave."

He comes back speedily. "She said okay. She still had her curlers on. But she's nice even when she gets out of bed." He looks at Heidi as he says it.

"Mrs. Henderson saves the day again." I sigh.

"Yeah. What would we do if she went to work?" Jeff says.

"Remember our keys or else." I look mean as I say it. "We need Mrs. Henderson. But she won't always be there."

"Got the message," Hans says.

Love . . . is not easily angered, it keeps no record of wrongs. Love does not delight in evil but rejoices with the truth. It always protects, always trusts, always hopes, always perseveres (1 Corinthians 13:4-7, NIV).

Those "Restful" Evenings

"I've got a ball game at six-thirty."
"And I have to be back at school by seven-thirty. Can you take me?"
"I need help with my math tonight. What's a 'real' number, anyway?"

Three requests. Three voices, almost simultaneous. They change our hope for a quiet evening. Jim and I look at each other as we get ready to put supper on, and he says to me, "You choose first."

"Definitely not the math," I say.

"Then you get the ball game. That's in half an hour."

Sure enough, it is. This is a good night for tomato soup and toasted cheese sandwiches fixed very fast. I take off my jacket which I've left on since work, shake off my shoes, and start hunting in the back of the refrigerator where I've hidden the cheese. My mind is still on something back at work, but I push those thoughts out of the way. I needed to rest, to clear my head, maybe even soak in a hot tub tonight, but that's got to wait.

Hans comes back downstairs in his white baseball suit. I

wonder where the tomato soup will land and try not to worry.

"Hope I get to play tonight," he says, punching his fist into his glove. "I've been warming up all afternoon."

"Wish you'd reminded me sooner about it," I say. "You could have called. That's twice now you've surprised me."

"It's on the calendar," he says. "In pink Magic Marker."

"Well, look at the calendar for me and remind me in the morning, then. I forget to look, you know."

"I know."

Jeff sets his math book down on the place mats as Jim opens a can of soup. "If you'll help me with this math right now," Jeff says, "I can come to the game, too."

Jim looks doubtful but sits down, spreading the silverware around as Jeff explains the problem. It's a word problem and until he figures out what it means, he can't work the math. Jim doesn't look ready for word problems himself.

"Just tell me how to do it," Jeff says.

"No. You tell me what it means first."

"Well, if I add sixteen and divide by thirty-two, is that my answer?" He points to his paper.

"No. That's not what the problem asks for," Jim sighs. "Read it again."

Jeff frowns. "Why do they have to make it so hard?"

"It's for life," Jim says. "Life is like that. First you have to figure out what something means. Then you get to use your math on it, once you understand."

"You always make the explanations too complicated," Jeff complains. "Just tell me how to write it down."

I look at the clock. The math lesson will not be over in time for the ball game. "Save it," I say. "We have to eat first. You'll have to move the books so that I can set the plates down."

Heidi brings her biology notes to the table. In her pocket is the scene from a play she has to memorize by a seven-thirty rehearsal.

"The game won't be over by seven-thirty," I tell her. "You'll have to bring your notes to the game, and I'll run you to school between innings." The games have been running two hours. Beginners' speed.

"Growl," she says. Then, "Okay. Maybe I can yell for Hans while I study."

Hans's face lights up. "She's serious. She'll yell for me. Thanks," he says.

"Sorry you have to miss the game," I say to Jim as we clear off the plates. Jeff's already back to the math book and looking up at Jim for help. There are nine more problems.

Jim winks at me. "We'll be done before you get home," he says. "Maybe I'll even get a nap."

"Terrific," I say. "You don't mind clearing up the kitchen, do you?"

He doesn't. He's fairly good at it.

As we head out the door, he winks again. "See you after my nap."

Evenings. A full-time occupation just getting through them. "Naps are for old age. I'll talk to you at ten," I say, "if everything's done by then."

"I'll save you a word problem," he says.

"That's okay. You can go to the game next time. That's Thursday, by the calendar."

Do everything in love (1 Corinthians 16:14, NIV).

 # Vacation Blues

Dear Lord, do you know everyone's on vacation except me?

The children have been off for three weeks already, and they have nine more to go.

Next week my husband starts a month of vacation, and he's going to England for ten days.

I've got one week the end of this summer and one at Christmas. That's all.

I tell it all as if the Lord doesn't know that. But I'm the one who has to get used to the information. I'm poring over camp catalogs and summer recreation programs and hoping the children can manage. This working thing is easy only when the children are in school. Already they say they're bored.

"Heidi," I say. "How are we going to make it until September?"

"Oh, Mom. Don't worry about it."

"Tell me one reason why not."

"Well, first, there's peanut butter. The miracle food. And then there's toasted cheese. Jeff's pretty good at those." She grins. "And then . . ." I see her trying to be more convincing. "And then . . . How old do you think we are, anyhow?"

My answer: "Fourteen, twelve, ten. Almost fifteen, thirteen, eleven."

"Well, see how simple it is?"

She flounces upstairs. Subject settled. She looks back into my somber face. "No problem!"

I sigh. To children life is always easy. I want to ask the Lord not to let them know that it isn't easy at all, but I don't ask. How will they manage their own children one day unless they know it isn't so simple?

"What if something happens?" I yell upstairs. "What if you needed me here?"

"We'd call you," she yells back. "You would come, wouldn't you?"

Hans bursts through the kitchen doorway. "Guess what?" he says. He's been on the telephone in the other room. "I'm going to be in a play. That was my teacher on the phone. She picked me, she said, because I'm so mature." He is an inch taller as he says it.

I look at his eyes, shining with pride in his new maturity. He's not counting the number of times he lost his key last year. Well, it was only once since March. Maybe he is better. If he'd only start turning out the lights upstairs, I'd call him mature, too. Maybe.

"The play's three mornings a week. That should keep me out of trouble."

"Yes, it should," I say. "Now if we can just get you signed up for swimming in the afternoons, maybe you won't have to be so bored."

"Sure," he says. "Sure. What are you frowning about, Mom?"

I've been frowning for two days. I'll stop it now because, "For every temptation there is a way of escape," says the Lord. I think I've just found the beginning of that way.

There hath no temptation taken you but such as is common to man: but God is faithful, who will not suffer you to be tempted above that ye are able; but will with the temptation also make a way to escape, that ye may be able to bear it (1 Corinthians 10:13).

Laundry Blitz

I think there's some magic to the way socks multiply and shirts mysteriously pile up in the laundry basket. If I empty it one night, it is half full and growing like a bowl of popcorn the next. I never actually see it fill up; so I'm sure some genie sneaks in at night and pulls dozens of socks and shirts out from under the beds. He seems to have an unending supply of them.

Or could it be Jeff? Come to think of it, he wore an old red shirt down to breakfast. It's his favorite and so old the seams are splitting. But when he went out the door to the bus, he was wearing green. After school, when he went outside to shoot baskets, his shirt was white with a red insignia on it. Then at bedtime I'm sure I saw him disappear for the night in an old yellow shirt. It could be Jeff.

I've never actually seen him change his socks more than once a day, but why is his pile of clean laundry always the biggest when we fold the laundry twice a week? Maybe he sleeps in an old pair of socks. That might explain it. Maybe that's what he does with the old ones with the holes in them.

I'm sure it's not Hans. We have to beg him to change his socks, and, until recently, he'd sleep in the same thing he wore all day if we didn't catch him at it. His folded laundry pile always seems smaller than anyone else's pile.

Heidi won't want to go on record about the mathematics of her white socks, but since some of hers are striped, she's definitely not the white sock and T-shirt genie. It's the laundry collection in the boys' hamper that does the magical appearing act in the early morning hours.

It's mysterious happenings like that that keep life humorous and light. I've got to look at the situation that way. It's one of life's minimal irritations. If I have to choose between too many socks or not enough, I suppose I'll encourage Hans to try to catch up with Jeff.

Meanwhile, right now, somewhere, the sock genie is making plans for his nightly invasion to pile up the socks and shirts for my amusement.

Be kindly affectioned one to another with brotherly love . . . (Romans 12:10).

Family Comforters

The worst has happened. I've made a mistake at work, and it will take me two or three days to rectify the damage so that I can face people again. I've called ahead to warn my family. I'm going to be miles away from everyone when I get home tonight, and it's not their fault.

"Hi, Mom," Heidi says when I come through the door. My palms are cold and my feet heavy and numb. I look at her and do not feel any movement in my face. She takes my coat without asking and hangs it in the closet—an amazing feat, since she has to be begged to hang her own coat. I barely think of that.

"I've set the table," she observes offhandedly. I see the best place mats, red roses in the center of the table, and crystal goblets set out. Something is simmering on the stove.

"Supper's in ten minutes," she says. "Sloppy Joes."

I look at the counter for the tell-tale tomato sauce and I don't see a drop. Everything's wiped up and the dishwasher is emptied and she's started reloading it. She moves around the kitchen quietly and fast, and if I weren't so numb, I would surely mention it. I've never seen her so efficient.

She sets the plates out on the counter, and Jim helps her

serve. She gives him directions about what kind of salad dressing she wants for the lettuce. He looks surprised at her, too.

The phone rings just before we sit down, and she grabs for it. Usually we'd have to wait for her to talk on the phone. But tonight she says very precisely, "Who's calling, please?" and "May I take a message?" and says to us when she hangs up, "They thought I was Mom."

No wonder. She's hardly herself tonight. Or else she's herself in some new way, the self she's getting ready to become.

I'm not hungry but I try to eat anyway, and I drink all the water from the crystal goblet. She watches to be sure I've enjoyed it. Her father compliments her. She pats him on the shoulder and clears off his plate.

Outside the sun sets across the hills in a red glow streaked by long, thin clouds. I sit at the table and look out the bay window at the colors, my chin in my hands.

Heidi takes my plate to the sink, and Jeff whisks off the place mats. I'm far away—out where the sun touches the hills for a moment—and I imagine the warmth of that touch.

Beside me at the table, Heidi pulls out a chair and sits down. She doesn't talk.

The orange sky thins and filters away, and in seconds it is dark. Heidi gets up again. She touches my arm. "Nobody's perfect," she says. "Just look at me."

She looks at the sky. "Out there somewhere . . . things are perfect out there . . . but I don't know . . . we just keep taking tests and doing homework. Sometimes A's. Sometimes F's. It just keeps on like that, doesn't it?"

I blink at her profundity, filling in the theology she has suggested as I stare out at the wisps of clouds filtering away in the dark. She's wise tonight. My teacher. And she reminds me of Paul whose theology is a help to me as I sit there in the stillness.

For now we see through a glass, darkly; but then face to face . . . (1 Corinthians 13:12).
For we that are in this tabernacle do groan, being burdened: not for that we would be unclothed, but clothed upon, that mortality might be swallowed up of life (2 Corinthians 5:4).

Disappointment

"You've got to come to school tomorrow morning at ten-thirty. Everyone's mom is coming. It's a news show, and I made the TV camera myself out of cardboard and black paper."

I can imagine just how clever Hans's camera is. He makes anything out of cardboard boxes. When we moved last time, he made three spaceships and two airports out of the boxes and two extra trucks out of shoe boxes. A few snips of the scissors and an imaginative eye and presto!—the transformation is startling. So I can imagine the camera.

And I can imagine, worse yet, the disappointment I'm about to see on his face because I can't come. We've moved and I've only been at this job three months. It's a desk job with numbers of letters to be gotten out. Sixteen other people would like to have had the job. I don't think I can ask for the privilege of a mid-morning break. I worry about those other people sometimes.

"I hate to tell you this, Hans," I begin, watching his face, "But I can't come. Not this time. I'm sorry."

He scowls and rips a paper he's been working on at the table. "Why not, Mom?"

"I can't get off work yet."

"How come everyone else's mom can come?"

"I guess they don't work, Hans. I'm surprised they'd have the program at ten-thirty in the morning. Don't they think fathers would like to see it, too?"

"Guess not."

"Your father would like to see it. I know he would."

"Well, then, I'll just ask him. Maybe he can come instead of you at ten-thirty. He's his own boss, isn't he?"

"Try him," I say.

I hear their discussion back in the study, and Hans comes back looking uncertain.

"Well?"

"He said he'd try to come. He said being your own boss means people are in your office all the time. He says he doesn't know if he can get away."

Hans kicks at the floor with his toe, and his eyes are down. "Why am I the only one?" he says.

"Are you?"

"Well, there's David. His mom's a lawyer. And Ricky. His mom works clear downtown. I guess that's all."

"Hans, I *want* to come," I plead. "I love the things you do. How can you help me to know what it's like?"

He hears my disappointment and relents. "Well," he says. "I *could* read you my news story. You could at least get to hear *me.*"

"You're the one I want to hear," I say. "Please read it to me."

He takes out his paper, jammed inside a schoolbook. As he stands in the middle of the kitchen an idea strikes him. "Tell you what," he says, "Maybe tomorrow night I can bring the camera home with me since I made it."

"Good idea," I say with relief. "We'll keep it up in your room."

He looks satisfied. He unrolls his paper and begins to read.

"The President announced today that he will eradicate—is that how you say that word—all international turmoil. . . ."

I listen to the big words and smile, imagining that I am sitting with those mothers as he says all those long words tomorrow. I wish I could be there. "That's good," I say, nodding at him. I applaud when he finishes and he bows.

"I'll pray for you tomorrow," I say. His eyes shine a minute, and we are both comforted by the thought.

"Thanks," he says. "Show you the camera later."

. . . *the God of all comfort . . . comforts us in all our troubles, so that we can comfort those in any trouble with the comfort we ourselves have received from God (2 Corinthians 1:3-4, NIV).*

# Future Manager

The telephone rings constantly after five o'clock, just when I'd like never to hear a phone again. At least only one out of five calls is for me.

Just in case the calls are for the two adults in the house, we insist that everyone in the family answer the phone in a particular way: not just, "H'lo," and dead silence, but, "Hello. Barcus residence." And then, "Who's calling, please?" or "May I take a message?"

Nothing is more annoying to me than a teenager on the other end of the phone who seems unwilling to give out a single word more than is required. I'm reluctant to call a house where a teenager lives. "Yes," "No," and "Don't know" just aren't enough response when someone is making an important call.

Tonight the phone is ringing for the sixth time. The odds are that it's for me, and I hear my voice being called. I didn't listen closely; so I hope Heidi sounded pleasant. I pick up the phone.

"Hello?"

The voice on the phone says, "I thought that was you answering the phone."

"No, my daughter," I say.

"Tell her she sounds about twenty-one," my caller says.

"I know she'll be delighted," I chuckle. That will be the best news of her day. She already claims she's ready to drive a car—immediately. The thought makes me cold. Answering a phone is one thing, I tell her. Driving is another.

I finish my call and pass the compliment on to her, then change the subject before she mentions the driving again.

"I'm glad you're off the phone," she says. "I've got to make some important calls. There's a youth retreat this weekend, and I want some information about it."

I listen to her dial the phone. "Hello," she says, explaining who she is and asking for the information. She has a pencil and paper by the telephone and is writing everything down and nodding her head. She is laughing a little and talking as if she's not at all shy or embarrassed. I admire her. I was afraid of adults at her age. Now she is thanking one person and dialing another number to start still another adult conversation, just as calm as she can be.

On Sunday one of the people she called looked for her in church. When I met him, a fortyish man from denominational headquarters, he said, "That's the most intelligent phone call from a young person I've had in a long time. You mean to say she's only fourteen?"

"Yes," I say. "Going on twenty-one."

"Where'd she learn to talk on the phone like she wasn't a kid?"

Heidi winks at me. She's heard the lecture about phone manners too many times.

"Maybe I should talk with her only by telephone after this," I say. But I laugh so as not to spoil the compliment.

She frowns a little, and I'm sorry I said it because the

incident is a signal that she intends to manage her own life without fear when the time comes. "Keep it up, Heidi," I whisper to her. She's strong and headed straight into the future.

"God has great things for this young lady," the gentleman standing before us says and shakes her hand.

She smiles, then runs over to her friends, fourteen just a little longer.

For you know that we dealt with each of you as a father deals with his own children, encouraging, comforting and urging you to live lives worthy of God, who calls you into his kingdom and glory (1 Thessalonians 2:11-12, NIV).

I'm Stubborn

Sometimes it's lonely being a working mother, especially when it's your day off and you've gone to a woman's coffee hour. The trouble is, no one else there is a working mother. You're a visitor from another world.

"You work?" someone says.

I nod and say where and that it's a day off; so I thought I'd come get acquainted.

"Too bad you can't come to 'sew and chat,'" someone says. "We meet every Tuesday."

I nod that it's too bad.

"I don't sew but I sure like to chat," she says.

I smile, not wanting to be unfriendly. I've forgotten how to spend a whole morning chatting. Sitting still for an hour without something to do makes me restless.

"My children," a neighbor at the other end of the table says, "are so helpless. If I weren't there in the mornings to get them off to school, I don't know what they'd do. Half the time they have to call me for something they forgot."

I'm silent. The comment is not directed at me, but I've raised the issue by coming here today.

"My Traci Ann spends so long on her hair that I have to take her to school myself. She just never gets to the bus stop on time."

I feel my blood running cold, and I sit very still. Heidi had better not miss the bus.

"My Anthony's just as bad. I don't know when he'll grow up. He never makes his bed because I can't stand to see him fuss with it. He said to me once, 'Mother, what do I need to learn this for anyhow? I'm just going to get married. I don't really need to learn to do it.'"

The neighbor on my right giggles. "And what did you say? That boy of yours is such a cutie."

"I said," she answered, "'When you're in college, you'll need to know how. I just can't come to college with you, Anthony.' And you know what he said? He's so dear I just couldn't think what to say. He said, 'Well, Mother, that's a long way off. So let's just forget about it.' I really laughed at him, especially when he said, 'You make Dad's bed, don't you? Why don't you just go on and make mine too?'"

I hear the laughter around me, friendly agreement to the helplessness of little boys. Someone asks a neighbor beside me, after a short pause to shift the train of thought, "And where is your daughter now? Is she married yet?" The girl in question is seventeen.

"No. But she's going with a boy in dentistry. A university boy."

"Lucky girl. She can go to all the big weekends."

"What's she studying?" I ask. "What are her *plans?*"

"Well, she'll take some practical courses in case she *has* to work. But if she marries this boy, she won't need to."

"Need to work?" I say, then realize that this is the wrong company in which to launch an impassioned defense of working or a defense of self-sufficient children.

I have some more cake, write down the recipe along with everyone else—far too sugary for me—and watch the clock.

At home my husband says, "That was good for you, dear. You're losing touch." He laughs at me.

I sigh agreement that it is good not to "lose touch." Then I give him the lecture I've been saving all day on self-sufficient children. After that I feel fine again.

Make it your ambition to lead a quiet life, to mind your own business and to work with your hands, just as we told you, so that your daily life may win the respect of outsiders and so that you will not be dependent on anybody (1 Thessalonians 4:11-12, NIV).

Out of Town

The more interesting the job, the greater the family complications are. Travel is the ultimate complication.

"Are you free to travel? Can you attend a conference on the west coast for us?" (That's one thousand miles away from *them*.)

Free? No, not free. None of us is free from one another in a family setting, but I'd love to go to the conference.

"I think I can manage it," I say (meaning, I think *they* can manage it).

"Can you be gone three days?"

"I'll work on it." (They'll work on it.)

Three days mean nine or ten meals planned in advance. Jim can cook them. So can Heidi. Jeff can do a lunch or two. And Hans is just starting in on cookies. I won't need to bake and freeze meals for a week before I go. I just need to make out a reasonable grocery list.

I'd like to turn the laundry off for a week, though. I ask for a slow-down at least. "Sure," everyone says, and I wonder how they will do it. I make sure Heidi knows how to run the washer. Jim knows how, but it would be nice if Heidi would do it.

Practicing, then. Will Hans practice his violin every night? "Aw, Mom," he says. "Give me a break."

"If it were summer, I would," I say. "But three days off in the middle of the week? Sorry. You keep a list every night, and I'll check it when I get back."

"Who's going to feed the dog at night?" I ask last. Jeff volunteers. He's most likely to remember; so I write him down for that. We've covered all the bases, I think. Nothing to do but wait.

I find it hard to wait. The convention is in Los Angeles, and I'll meet people from all over the country who are working on family legislation. I plan the next several days around that moment on the calendar when I will take the airport bus and actually be on my way.

An hour before it's time to go, I suddenly don't want to leave. The conference promises to be unforgettable. But the children—Jeff, quiet; Heidi, humming and not talking; Hans, outside as if I'd already gone—my image of their faces makes me know how much I will miss them. I'll call every night I vow. My steps are heavy as I kiss them each good-bye and finally climb on the bus heading for the airport. Jim waves good-bye from the bus depot and says they'll be "pros." Not to worry.

Once I'm in the air, I feel light again. My mind is racing ahead to the conference, and I'm checking the batteries in my cassette recorder to take down all the speeches. I won't call every night after all. Jim is there. They'll be fine. And they know where I am staying.

I look out at the blue sky laced with white clouds. I'm thousands of miles high in the air, racing toward the ocean, and I've got a job to do.

I'm free.

And I'm not free. I will love them every minute I'm away. We are gifts to each other from the Lord. Nothing will ever change that. Who shall separate us from the love of Christ?

. . . neither the present nor the future, nor any powers, neither height nor depth, nor anything else in all creation, will be able to separate us from the love of God that is in Christ Jesus our Lord (Romans 8:38-39, NIV).

Ordinary Mothers

"There are Bible verses that say you belong at home. Why don't you try it for a while?"

My friend has known me for a long time. We've said almost everything to each other and compared our differences. She's never worked—a matter of principle. Her children are models of obedience and orderliness. They practice for thirty minutes regularly and never raise their voices to their mother—at least they didn't until recently when they started into the two-digit ages. My friend thinks staying home with her children has made a big difference in the way they have turned out.

I agree she's done well, but I don't agree with her suggestion that I try it. The Bible, she reminds me, says to train the young women to be keepers at home. "It talks," she says, "almost exclusively about the woman's domain within the household."

I leaf through my Bible, looking for the exceptions. There was Mary who chose the better part over Martha, who was cumbered about with much serving. There was Deborah, a political leader, and Anna, the prophetess.

"Exceptions," my friend says. "Not the rule."

"Education," I remind her, "makes the difference today.

It's a different world. Of course, unschooled women should not presume to raise their opinions loudly in public. Of course, Paul wanted churches orderly so that he could preach the gospel. That was his first priority, the reason he wrote all those letters."

I see her about to break in, but I'm not through yet.

"Jesus," I add. "Take a close look at Jesus. Women haven't been the same since Jesus. He talked to women that no one else would even look at—the woman at the well, Mary Magdalene. He turned them into full-time professionals for his cause. There was something about Jesus that could do that."

My friend looks worried. "My job's at home," she says. "I've got more verses on my side than you do on yours. You're just working with *implications*. I've got the solid evidence."

"Ah, but those implications," I say. "The Scripture is full of them. 'In Christ there is neither Greek nor Jew, male nor female.' Or how about Paul's prayer that every believer find the 'breadth, length, depth, height, fullness of Christ.' How about that one? God never gave us gifts of intellect, creativity, and communication only to let us squander them. 'To whom much is given, much is expected.' We've got better choices today. Surely those Scripture verses you've got on your side don't mean we should be half-able, half-mature, half-adult. I know too many women who use your verses for an excuse."

She flinches and I am sorry.

"I don't mean you," I say. "You're good at this." I gesture toward her clean house, her home-sewn clothes, the cherry pie on her counter. "You've got talent. You read books, too, and you're the best church school teacher at Greenbranch Church."

"You could be, too," she whispers softly. "Why don't you give it a chance?"

"Because," I say, trying not to show my impatience, "I don't want to. One thing about God I've noticed is that God doesn't push people against the grain. You've got to understand mè, JoAnn."

I square off and stare at her. "God made me with this restlessness—this need to be doing something more—and God means to fulfill it. I'm happy when I'm busy. I think it's in my blood. My mother was that way, too. And God knows that."

"Stay home," JoAnn pleads. "Be sure, Nancy. *There*. I'll never say it again. But I had to say it."

We part friends. I respect her for speaking her mind. I like women who can say what they think without getting angry.

At supper that night I repeat her conversation. Heidi's eyes fly open and she says, "I hope you didn't take all that seriously, Mother. I can't imagine you'd let her talk you into it."

Jeff just looks at me to see what I say I will do.

Jim, sensible husband that he is, just looks at me too, smiling out of the corners of his eyes. Finally he says, "What would we do with you—home all day? You'd probably write more unpublishable novels than anyone in history. I'm sure you wouldn't get back into heavy dusting or window washing."

Hans waits his turn. I can see he has an opinion. "Well," he finally says. "I would like it if you got home a little sooner to make me a snack. But I never really liked popcorn anyway, come to think of it. So don't let that stop you. Besides," he says, rolling his eyes, "you're more my type this way."

He waits for my smile, then rushes on, one more point to make. "Whatever you do," he says seriously, his eyes steady on me for a moment and trying not to twinkle with his mischief, "I sure hope you won't be one of those *ordinary mothers!*"

"I'll be whatever God tells me to be," I say quietly.

"Let's pray," Jim says and we close our eyes.

. . . the God of our Lord Jesus Christ, the Father of glory, may give unto you the spirit of wisdom and revelation in the knowledge of him: The eyes of your understanding being enlightened; that ye may know what is the hope of his calling, and what the riches of the glory of his inheritance in the saints. . . . (Ephesians 1:17-18).